Warrior Within:
Healing Childhood Abuse
The Inner Child Emotional
Intelligence & Boundaries

Warrior Within: Healing Chilhood Abuse Book 2

Warrior Within

Mike Bowles

Published by Mike Bowles, 2024.

WARRIOR WITHIN: HEALING CHILHOOD ABUSE BOOK 2

First edition. March 3, 2024.

ISBN: 979-8224436002

Written by Mike Bowles.

" I have been fighting to survive since I was a child,
I am not a survivor
I am a warrior"
-unknown

Foreword

Sexual abuse of children is something that is both writhe in society and very taboo.

An estimated one in every four girls and one in six boys are sexually abused at least once before their eighteenth birthday. For most of these children though, they are abused multiple times and over a period of time by their perpetrator.

Many of these crimes will go unreported by the child until late adulthood (if ever reported at all). This leads the individual to develop a vast number of personal and interpersonal struggles. Lack of trust in others, low self esteem, lack of self worth, relationship issues and issues creating boundaries are to name a few, not to mention that mental health conditions that sexual abuse trauma creates such as severe depression and anxiety, post traumatic stress disorder and borderline personality disorder to name but a few. When an abuse survivor begins to come to terms with the historic abuse they encountered in their childhood, they are offered medication for mental health issues and are offered therapy sessions to deal with their past traumas. But as well as dealing with current mental health and past traumatic experiences, at some point a survivor must also adopt a more holistic approach to their healing in order to overcome their poor self esteem and negative self view to go forward and live a fuller and happier life. The learning, practice and incorporation of skills into a survivor's daily life are essential to them building a life after dealing with a traumatic past.

In this series of self help books I will share with you the daily practices that I discovered and incorporated into my own healing journey that allowed me to overcome my

own experiences of childhood sexual abuse, emotional abuse and neglect.

Learning about the practices in these books, and more importantly putting them into consistent practice in daily life, you will also be able to overcome the devastating effects that can overshadow a survivor's entire life.

Almost all survivors I have met in person and online via chat groups and forums have told me the same thing. They get help in therapy sessions for dealing with the past, but do not get help to move forward into the future, which keeps them held in a place of always healing, but never being healed because they do not know or have been shown how to move forward.

If you are tired of feeling stuck and tormented by the events of your past then start by learning and using the practices in these books to get your life back.

Note: The exercises in this book are not meant to replace professional therapy, but to be used alongside professional help you heal from the trauma of childhood abuse.

The Inner Child

'If I could go back in time I would tell my little self…
You are beautiful,
You are perfect,
You are loved'
-Katrina Mayer

One of the areas I have struggled with for most of my life, is the understanding, feeling and acceptance of my own emotions. This is something that has shadowed my life both at times when I have denied and blocked out my abuse and when I have even come to terms with it. My emotional range would generally consist of either being completely turned off and numb and not allowing myself to really feel anything, or to anger and frustration. Not the sort of anger where I would rage or shout or argue, but the kind where I could be short with people, or abrupt, or very ' matter of fact and that's the end of that conversation, thank you very much'. In a lot of ways I could be very uncompassionate towards people and believe that it's my way or no way. For many years, I kept my walls up and people out and that is the way it was staying. As you can imagine having that kind of attitude in life doesn't really gain you many friends and it doesn't allow you to have those meaningful relationships. For many years I would tell myself that I didn't need other people, I didn't want other people and that I was better off in my own little bubble. I think many suvivors of child abuse tell themselves the exact same thing. After all, if we don't let people in, we cannot get hurt again right. That stands to reason.

What we fail to acknowledge though is that the heartache of being lonely hurts just as much, if not more in the long run.

But that is something that we do not let ourselves acknowledge. At least I didn't. I kept that inner pain of being lonely. That need of wanting a family, of wanting a mum and a dad a best friend - buried. Buried deep. Sometimes I used to imagine what it would be like to have those connections, but then I would also immediately put myself back in that place of secure confinement.

So why do we do this? Why do we find it easier to block people out than to let people in?

Because it is easier ? Because it is familiar? Maybe. Partly.

But the real answer is shame. It is the shame that we experienced in childhood that taught us how to hide and block our emotions. We learned how to hide the sorrow and fear that we encountered as a child in order to learn how to survive at the time. Because we were abused, rejected and hurt in childhood we grew up learning and embedding how to lock away all that pain. Much like in Book 1, where I described how the brain blocks the memory to safeguard us, our emotional development also becomes blocked (or sheltered) to protect us. Our brain wants us to feel as little pain as possible and so not feeling emotions is another way it reduces that risk. The problem is we learned how to lock away all the good emotions as well through fear of not getting hurt further along with numbing off the unwanted For me, not only was I abused by a family member, I was also let down and neglected by the people who were supposed to care for me the most - my parents. So I learned, like many survivors did, that it is easier not to let anyone in because that way I cannot get hurt.

I have come to learn though, much like how the brain will eventually allow you to start to remember the events, the heart will also start to yearn for connection. This can manifest itself in many ways and often without us even realising it happens. For me, one of the biggest ways that it has always manifested itself without me even realising is by finding myself replacement parents. I have seen at least two of my bosses as father figures and looked for validation and acceptance and even seeked parental guidance from them. I have worked tirelessly (to my own detriment) to make them proud of me. However, when they have had to leave either due to a change of career or promotion, I have then felt let down, abandoned and rejected. I have even done the same with women that have come into my life and have looked at people I work with and have sometimes in the past looked at girlfriends mums and wished they were mine.

But as well as feeling shut off or trying to replace family members that emotional disconnect can also manifest itself in other ways such as -

- Depressions and Anxiety

- Anger Management issues

- Passive Aggressive behaviour

- Low self esteem

- Abandonment issues

- Borderline Personality Disorder (also called Emotionally Unstable Personality Disorder)

- Emotional Numbness

- Self Sabotage

- Self Criticism

- Codependency and powerlessness

One of the ways in which we can overcome emotional numbness, or at least get reconnected, with our emotion is to do something called 'Inner Child' work (or 'Shadow work' as it is sometimes called).

When I first heard of Inner Child work, I didn't fully grasp the concept of it. I was of the impression that I am now an adult. Why on earth would I want to work on my inner child? I did not have a great childhood, so why on earth would I want to revisit that ? First she asked me if I blame myself for the abuse. She knew that I did. We have often had conversations in the past where I had told her about certain incidents and that I should have 'run at that point', or I 'should have spoken up then' because if I had it would not have been as bad. I would sit in sessions describing elements of my abuse that I could not get out of my head and tell her how if I had done something different I could have stopped it. I would blame myself. So I told her 'Yes' of course I blame myself. She then went on to ask me that if a child came in the room right now and told me that what happened to me was happening to them would I look them in the eye and tell them it was their fault? She knew full well the answer was no, but her point was that we work with the inner child because we not only are that when we suppress that emotional development, but also because we can take away the ability to self blame and in many ways self sabotage the healing process.

(And yes, just as a side note, as survivors we can and do in fact self sabotage the healing process. We can become so binded to the thought of self blame that any new way of thinking and healing must be wrong. Ultimately our way of shutting people out, shutting down and blocking everything has kept us alive, so in many ways it is a good thing. It stems from that tension dynamic described in Book 1)

What exactly is the inner child ?

The term 'inner child' doesn't mean that there is a little kid living inside of you or that there is part of your brain that is solely assigned to childish thoughts. The general idea is that we all have a childlike aspect to our personality, in both positive and negative ways. It is the part of us that has a temper tantrum when we cannot get our own way. It is also the part that likes to watch Disney animated films even though we are really too old. It is the part that likes to play and get involved in a water fight or that doesnt even like sharing that last piece of cake. The inner child is part of a 'sub personality' that we all have. However, for victims of childhood abuse, it is part of us that we can very much lock away. For most people who have not encountered abuse, they have a natural emotional development and transition from child through to adolescent through to young adult and then adult. Survivors however tend to almost stop that emotional transition at around the age they were traumatised. Instead of being able to process emotional responses and have that natural transition, we tend to suppress those emotions in order to survive. That does not mean that they are not there though, it just means that we have to work at accessing them and it is the getting in contact and accessing of silenced emotions of the inner child that also helps us heal from our past.

There are many outcomes for connecting with the inner child as well that are all beneficial to a survivors these include -

- Accessing repressed memories and emotions
- Being able to feel after years of feeling numb
- Regaining personal power and be able to set boundaries
- Learn how to take better care of yourself
- Self compassion

- Liking yourself more
- Increased self confidence
- Being able to enjoy life and have fun

When I first started inner child work, one of the tasks that Carol gave me was to write to my inner child. What she advised me to do was to think of myself at an age when the abuse was occurring and when I was feeling really lost in the world. She advised me to get a picture of myself at that age if I could. I couldn't. I didn't really have any contact with my family or anyone who would have had pictures of me at that age. In all honesty, I would be surprised if any actually existed. But if you are going to do this exercise and you do have access to a picture, then you may find it helpful to connect to yourself. My homework for that particular session was that Carol wanted me to write a letter to my child self. I chose the age of nine years old the first time I did this. I didn't really know what to write or how to address my nine year old self so I wrote down what I remembered from life at that age. I wrote down how I remembered living with my mum. How I had to live with my aunt for a little while whilst I was a ward of court. How I went to London and visited the High Court whilst my parents were fighting a custody battle and how my mum told me that she had lost and dumped me on my dad's doorstep(She hadn't actually told me she lost the court case until we knocked on his door. I thought I was visiting for the weekend,but it turned out I was now living there) and I wrote about my first encounter of sexual abuse. I wrote a letter to myself that ended up being about twenty sides of A4 paper long initially. After I was happy with the letter, or felt I had written enough, the next part of the task was to reply to myself. I had to read the letter in its entirety and reply to myself as though

I was that child. It seemed a very peculiar thing to do at first, but the trick was not to reply as an adult, it was to reply from that inner child viewpoint. I had to reply while being and feeling connected to all the emotions that I was feeling back then. Something that helped with this (a little tip from Carol) was to write the reply with my non dominant hand. As I completed this exercise I began to notice a lot of emotion come flooding in. I had gone very quickly from an adult viewpoint of mostly feeling numbed off to emotion and an attitude of ' I should have done more to stop it' to remembering and feeling what I did at nine years old.. I worked through each aspect of the letter and how I felt at every step. I wrote about how I was feeling so scared and alone as I had to go and live with an aunt that I didn't know. How I was so confused about everything that was going on throughout the court case. How I felt that no one was listening to me or that I wanted to stay with my mum. I remembered how much I cried the day my mum dropped me off to live with my dad and that sudden realisation that it wasn't for a visit but for good. I felt so betrayed that day. She never told me what was going on, we just pulled up on the road my dad lived down. We walked to his front door with a bin liner of my clothes, knocked on the door and she said the words 'You live here now'. I wrote about how truly alone I felt in that first week at my new home and I wrote about how we went to visit my dad's side of the family that first weekend. I remembered as we visited my Nans house and then to aunts and uncles that lived close by how I sat there, in solace. There was never a ' Mike do you remember your aunt' (or cousin or whoever) by my dad. I was just told to go in and sit down and be quiet. None of these people spoke to me. Until I got to my oldest cousin's house. He was sixteen. Out of all the family members that I had met that day (re met) , he was the only one that took an interest. At first it was he just him asking simple things like 'Do you want to play in the garden?', 'Do you want to walk to the shop with me?'.Simple things. After a long period of people not really telling me what was going on or really speaking to me at all, especially throughout the custody battle, it was nice to just have someone to talk to. A friend. That was until he asked me if I wanted to go up to his room to look at his Star Trek stuff. That was where I remember freezing as he put my hands down his pants and squeezed my hand around his erection. I wrote about all the feelings that I had when I went back home that day. How I just felt shocked and confused and truly alone in the world.

You see, when you start to write your reply from your inner child, you become a lot more emotionally connected to yourself. You suddenly find a level of self compassion that was previously lost. That ability to blame yourself for not doing 'more' or doing 'something' to stop it starts to fade. Connecting with that inner child can also have other outcomes as well. As you begin to write from your younger self's viewpoint, you also start to remember a lot more of what was happening to the time, which in turn also allows you to see more of the bigger picture and who WAS to blame.

I have now done this exercise a few times. Throughout my healing journey I have felt the need to contact my inner child at three key points in my life. Or at least three different versions of a younger me. As well as that nine year old, I have also gotten in contact with a five year old me. The child who really needed and was desperate for motherly love, guidance and protection. At that age my parents had not long gone through a divorce and I had gone from having two parents, two sisters and a brother, to my family being ripped apart and it being me, my mum and her (physically abusive) new boyfriend. I also felt the need to get in contact with a teenage me. The fifteen year old who was very confused and hurt. Who had not only been being abused on a regular basis by his cousin, but was neglected by both parents, and raped. Who was confused about sex, sexuality, love and who couldnt even make out when he lost his virginity. Each and every time I have done this exercise, I have gotten closer to myself, and my emotions. And each time a step closer to healing.

There are also other ways to contact your inner child. Whilst letter writing (or even journalling), from that child's viewpoint and emotions is a great way to reconnect with your past trauma, it is also important to also balance that out with reconnecting with the joyful side of your inner child. The playful part of that subpersonality that also dreams. There are a variety of ways to do this, but mine is to just play. One of my favourite toys as a kid was always Lego. I used to love building things from imagination and creatively playing. So as an adult, I bought myself some Lego in order to help reconnect with the positive emotions and connect with a happier child version of me. I also used to love watching Thundercats as a kid, so I found a retro boxset on Ebay; and I can even be found climbing trees when we visit the park. Getting in contact with that adventurous and imaginative side of your inner child is just as important to healing as dealing with the trauma. Not only do we need to revisit our inner child to find that emotional connection, sometimes we need to revisit in order to re discover our hopes, dreams and inner joy

Contacting our inner child can be a very revealing practice to go through. For a lot of people it usually brings about a new level of understanding of self compassion and an understanding of our emotions. It allows us to in many ways parent ourselves. But, doing inner child work can also bring other revelations. For some it helps reveal and remember repressed childhood memories as well as the attached emotions. It can also increase your level of self compassion and self care and it can also help survivors identify and overcome unhealthy patterns such as going from toxic relationship to toxic relationship as an adult.

Emotional Intelligence

Use pain as a stepping stone, not a camp ground."
- Alan Cohen
"When awareness is brought to an emotion, power is brought to your life."
– Tara Meyer Robson
"We cannot tell what may happen to us in the strange medley of life. But we can decide what happens in us — -how we can take it, what we do with it —- and that is what really counts in the end."
—

- Joseph Fort Newton

What is Emotional Intelligence?

Emotional Intelligence is not something that I came across directly on my healing journey. It wasn't one of the methods or theories or practices that I had looked at in books or online or in therapy or on courses. I first came across the term 'Emotional Intelligence' through my career.. I was working for a large retail company as a store manager and was learning and developing to climb the corporate ladder. This was long before I had my breakdown or even acknowledged my traumatic past. Part of my development was to attend a two year long in house course called the Leadership Improvement Programme. That was broken down into Coaching Others, Business Building and The biggest part - Emotional Intelligence. The emotional intelligence part of the course was all about firstly getting to truly understand yourself. What makes you tick and how to understand why you respond and behave the way that you do to people and in situations. But it also taught me how to recognise those things in other people (What makes them tick, what motivates them and the why of their response). This greater understanding of 'self' and emotional intelligence is something that I revisited after I started recalling my childhood trauma. It was when I was trying to find who I was (when I had lost my identity) that I rediscovered the work books and notes that I had kept from my time taking that development course . I'm not sure if it was fate, coincidence or an inner knowing or where my workbooks on the subject were, but something led me to finding the work I had done years ago on self identity when I needed it the most. I was clearing the loft and came across an old suitcase full of all my leadership and coaching materials that I had kept from work. I had loads of workbooks and exercises and notes on things such as delegation and time management and a number of other management and leadership skills that I used to teach new managers and supervisors. In that suitcase, amongst all my books (actually they were sitting on top), were all my emotional Intelligence books. I started rereading them and doing the exercises, but instead of doing them with the viewpoint of improving my leadership skills, I looked at them from the lack of self identity that had incurred since having a breakdown over my childhood abuse. After re doing a lot of the work, it did bring me closer to not only realising who I am, but also gave me a renewed strength on how to move forward and deal with certain aspects of the abuse and some of the people that were related to the abuse.

It is this greater understanding and discovery of self that I am going to get you to do.

In order to move forward from abuse, (and to grow as people)we need to grow our emotional intelligence. This is often something that is developmentally hindered by our abuse and can lead us to have extreme reactions to people. Often the sense of true self is lost inside us and trying to seperate that out from learned behaviour and the needs of the inner child can be confusing. In many ways this leads on perfectly from any Inner child work that you may (should have) done in connecting with your emotions.

In the following exercise (and I pre warn you, it is a long exercise that you may need to do over a period of time and re read and revisit an number of times), we are going to learn about how to identify our true self, how to identify our emotional intelligence, find our values, draw boundaries and identify and deal with toxic people.

<u>Getting to know you</u>

Back in 460BC (ish) a guy called Hippocrates was born. He is commonly known as the father of modern medicine and was the first to dismiss the belief that illness was caused by evil spirits or the fate of the gods, but was a physical problem in the body itself/ he was the first to theorise that thoughts and feelings came from the brain and not the heart. He was also the first to notice that people had different behavioral traits - which he believed was caused by different levels of bodily fluids. Hippocrates saw a basic four behavioural which he described as Choleric. Sanguine, Phlegmatic and Melancholic. He then went on to group together the types of behaviour these types of people could be predicted to show. This part of the course uses the 4 basic traits to help you understand yourself and others.

For the purpose of learning, we are going to give colors to the four personality traits - are you a Fiery Red, Sunshine Yellow, Earthy Green or Cool Blue? Mostly because my inner child would rather deal with colors.

There is no right or wrong color to be. None is better or stronger than the other; they are just all different from each other. Each one has its own strengths and weaknesses and whilst will find that you have qualities of all 4 color types - you will have one that is your dominant personality type and how you are comfortable being.

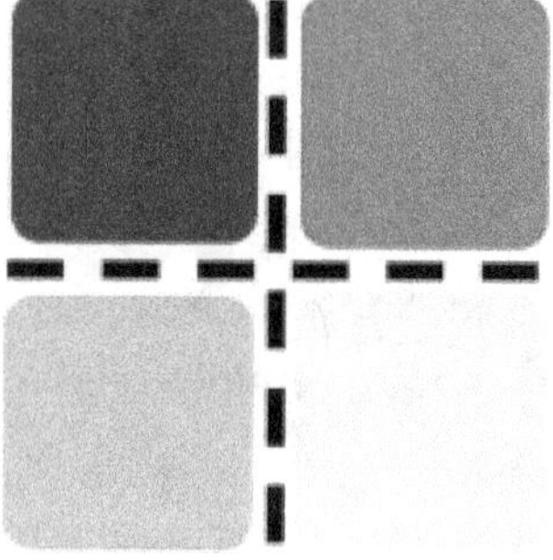

To discover what is your most dominant trait, there are a series of self tests that we can do. It is not uncommon for us to think we are one thing because of learned behaviour, only to find we are actually something different.

Introversion vs Extraversion

YOUR ATTITUDE
  INTROVERSION EXTRAVERSION
  QUIET - or - TALKATIVE
  OBSERVANT - or - INVOLVED
  INWARD FOCUS - or- OUTWARD FOCUS
  DEPTH FOCUSED - or -BREADTH FOCUS
  INTIMATE - or - GREGARIOUS
  RESERVED - or -FLAMBOYANT
  REFLECTIVE - or- ACTION ORIENTATED
  THOUGHTFUL - or - OUTSPOKEN
  CAUTIOUS - or -BOLD
  Do you feel you have a more Introvert or Extravert attitude?

Thinking VS Feeling

The next step to finding your true self is to find out if you use your head (think) or your heart (feel) in situations. Again, because we can get lost in feeling a lot of pain and inner anguish, we can be tempted to believe that we are FEELING people. But this is not the case.

A typical THINKING preference would be to step OUT if situations to analyse the reason and logic from a distance

A typical FEELING preference would be to step INTO a situation and get a feel for the value and motives

You will use both, but one is more natural. The natural style for you, is the one you react with, without thinking about it.

Thinking

Thinkers like to use Logic and apply cause & effect principles when dealing with people and emphasize a task orientation when dealing with people.

A thinker would look for the solution to the problem, with the focus being on analysing the problem and looking for the logical solution.

Feeling

Feeling people are driven by values and conviction. They look for harmony within other people, want common ground and like to treat people individually.

They like to be appreciated for who they are . If they are helping a friend with a task, they would emphasize the problem and focus on how the friend was feeling about the problem and support them to feel better about things.

A really quick test of this is this-

A family member or friend has borrowed your car. They have just phoned you to say that they have had an accident. What is the FIRST thing you would say is it

   A. Have you gone to the hospital ?
   B. Are you hurt?
   C. Is there much damage?
   D. Do you need me to come to you?

Now you may very well ask all four questions, but it is the one you ask first that will give a good indication of whether you are really a thinker or a feeler. 'Have you gone to the hospital?' and ' Is there much damage?' are both THINKING questions. They are both questions that are about logical things that need to be done. ' Are you hurt ?' and ' Do you need me to come to you?', are FEELING questions. They are ones that are concerned with the other person. Remember, there is no right or wrong answer, as I say you may ask all four questions, but it is the initial question that you ask will give you an idea if you are that thinking personality or that feeling personality type. Thinkers will lead with their head, Feelers will lead with their heart.

You can also test yourself with this in daily life. Think about recent conversations that you have had or when people have confided in you. What is the first thing you have said? Does it fall in the realm of a logical step to take or to comfort the other person?

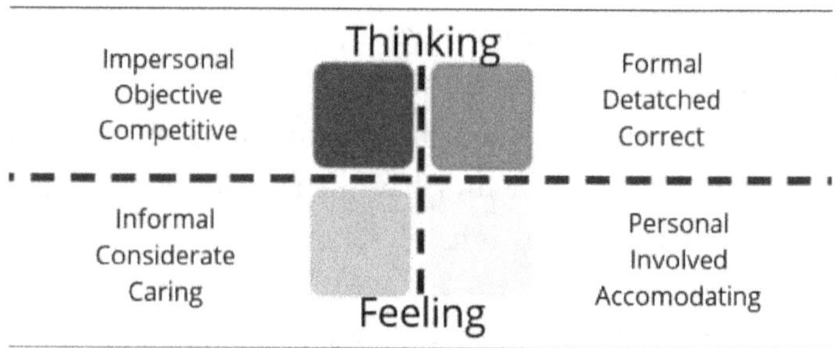

Read the Statements below and mark on the scale which one you feel is closer to your personal preference. Look at your choices. Are they closer to Thinking or Feeling ?

<u>YOUR DECISION MAKING FUNCTIONS</u>

Thinking Feeling

FORMAL - or - INFORMAL

IMPERSONAL - or - PERSONAL

ANALYTICAL - or - ILLOGICAL

DETACHED - or - INVOLVED

OBJECTIVE - or - SUBJECTIVE

STRONG MINDED - or - FLEXIBLE

COMPETITIVE - or- ACCOMODATING

PARTICULAR - or - AMBIVALENT

TASK FOCUSED - or - RELATIONSHIP FOCUSED

Do you have a **THINKING** or **FEELING** preference?

Activity :

In the space below, write about a Snowman. (We will come back to this later,but for now write as much or as little a Snowman as you like)

SENSING VS INTUITION

SENSING

If your attention is focused on taking in reality of information (what it says on the label) - factual and practical information given by the five senses, then you are SENSING

Sensing people will focus on what is real and actual. They value practical application. They are factual and can remember specific things, conversations and information. Enjoy the present time and like information to be accurate.

They will state what they can see and look to describe the detail of what is front of them with clarity. They will follow instructions to complete a task and be sure they are doing it the correct way.

INTUITION

People who use intuition will focus on 'big picture' possibilities. They value imagination and see patterns and meanings behind the information. They enjoy creative thinking. They prefer to think beyond the reality of what is in front of them and consider other possibilities, going wherever their imagination takes them. They improvise and are energised by doing things their way.

<u>Your Working Preferences</u>

<u>**Sensing Intuition**</u>
SPECIFIC - or -OPEN ENDED
DETAILED -or- _RANDOM
ORDERLY - or- ABSTRACT
FACTUAL - or- OPINION
LOGICAL - or- ILLOGICAL
PAST - or - FUTURE
EXPERIENCE - or - OPPORTUNITIES
CONVENTIONAL - or- EXCITING
EXACT - or - FLEXIBLE

Do you have a Sensing preference or Intuitive preference?

If you are still not sure, look back at what you wrote about a snowman. Did you write the basics about a snowman? That it is s white, has a hat and scarf, coal eyes and so on. Or did you start to add in extra like he was happy or had coloured hat and colourful scarf. Did you start to give your snowman a bit of a backstory in your head or on paper? Sensing people would have kept to the facts about a snowman. Intuitive people would have given him more character .

Now that you have a better understanding of what drives you, you should be able to identify which one of the 4 core personality types is your primary.

Mark on the grid below, which color you are using the information from the previous charts.

If you are are Extravert that Thinks and is Intuitive - you are a Red personality type

If you are an Extravert that Feels and is Sensing - you are a Yellow personality type

If you are an Introvert that Thinks and is Intuitive - you are a Blue Personality type

I you are an Introvert that Feels and is Sensing- you are a Green Personality type

So, why is this information important or relevant?

Well, in order to heal, it is important to know what we are dealing with; and the best way for us to heal ourselves is to know ourselves. For example, I am a Blue personality type. I like facts and things to do. I like to know exactly what is up and the best course of action to take to fix a problem. Going into therapy, this is very useful for me to know because I can (and did) outline exactly what I needed. Yes I needed to talk and an unbiased ear to listen, but I also needed logical actionable steps to take. To me, every problem has a solution so show me the solution and I'll work it out. I could tell Carol, my therapist, that I needed things to work on and activities to help me heal and she could provide them. I know that a lot of people are asked by their therapists ' What do you need from me?' and quite often our answer is ' I don't know'. Knowing yourself and doing this exercise may help you a little with that and outlay some of your expectation of therapy. For example if you are a Green personality - a person that is introverted and feeling, you will have your personality type respected. You will need and want your therapist to primarily be very caring and on your level - perhaps sit next to you in therapy rather than opposite. A green personality type would not get on with a very 'clinical' therapist that makes no eye contact or displays no emotion and keeps telling them what they need to do . However on the flip side a red personality type would much prefer the clinical style therapist, whereas if they had a therapist that sat close and showed the same amount of empathy that a green person would require, they would quickly become disengaged in the process.

When you look at the previous diagram you will see that Red and Green and Blue and Yellow are opposite each other. Green people are generally very caring and gentle and much more considerate of another person's feelings. A Red person, who is a Greens opposite are very much action orientated people. They prefer to just be direct and to the point. Blue people are very logical and analytical people who focus on detail , whereas their opposing Yellows like to be creative and wild and erratic. Interestingly, we generally marry a person that is either the same personality type as us, or the polar opposite .

Fill In the following

Self Analysis - What is your preferred color type?

How does it compare with :

Your Spouse -

Your Parents -

Your Therapist -

Other significant people in your life?

The following chart demonstrates some of the qualities and traits of each personality type. How do these traits fall in with the characteristics that You have given to people in your previous exercise.? Do they align?

Colour
Summary

Personality Preference	Indirect Non- Emotive	Indirect Emotive	Direct Emotive	Direct Non Emotive
Attitude type	Introverted Thinking	Introverted Feeling	Extraverted Feeling	Extraverted Thinking
Appears	Formal Conservative Structured	Casual Conforming Personal	Fashionable Stylish Stimulating	Business Like Functional Busy
Work Preference	Organised Functional Formal	Relaxed Friendly Informal	Personal Cluttered Friendly	Formal Efficient Structured
Style	Slow/ Systematic	Slow/ Easy	Fast/ Spontaneous	Fast/ Decisive
Focus	Task & Process	Maintaining Relationship	Interacting/ Relationships	Task/ Results
Fears	Embarrassment	Confrontation	Loss of Prestige	Loss of Control
When under tension wil	Withdraw / Avoid	Submit	Attack / be sarcastic	Dictate / Assert
Like	Accuracy	Attention	Recognition	Productivity
Is concerned with	How to logically Justify How things work	How it will affect their personal circumstance	How it enhances their status	What it does By when What i s the cost
Seeks security in	Preparation	Close Relationships	Flexibility	Control
Wants to	Credibility	Relationships	Status	Success

maintain

Helps

Support

	Analysis	Warmth	Relationships	Objectives
Seeks to achieve acceptance through	Correctness Thoroughness	Conforming Loyalty	Playfulness Stimulating the environment	Leadership Competitiveness
Like you to be	Precise	Pleasant	Outgoing	Brief
Wants to be	Correct	Liked	Admired	In control
Is irritated by	Surprises Unpredictability	Insensitivity Impatience	Boredom Routine	Inefficiency Indecision
Measure Personal Worth	Precision Accuracy Activity	Compatibility with others Depth of one relationship	Recognition Applause Compliments	Results Track Record Measurable Progress
Decisions are	Paced and deliberate	Considered	Spontaneous	Quick and Decisive

As with all personality types, they have positive and negative sides to them, Here are some traits that each color may display if they are having a bad day or are being negative

RED

The negative traits of a Red personality are that they may be quite destructive, have temper tantrums if they cannot get their own way. They can be increasingly rude, blunt and abrupt and very quick to react.

YELLOW

These people will show their negative characteristics in a very loud way. If they are upset, they will want everyone to know about it . They may be overly dramatic and retaliate with mean and offensive sarcasm. These guys like to play the blame game when stressed

BLUE

Blue people when upset or being negative will resort to facts and figures. They will look for more and more information as to why they are right and you are wrong, and try to force them on you as much as possible. To the point that they will tie you up in knots and confuse you.

GREEN

The greens are the most likely to cry when upset. They are also the ones that will hold a long term grudge and in times of difficulty will bring stuff into an argument that happened years ago and is irrelevant to the conversation. They are the ones that are most likely to be in a negative state of mind for the longest after something has upset them

Emotional Intelligence

Now that you understand a bit more about personality types, we can use this to build our emotional intelligence, which is an important factor when it comes to dealing with other people in your life. Whether it is building positive relationships or dealing with toxic people in your life and having to build boundaries, being aware of and practicing emotional intelligence skills is invaluable.

Emotional Intelligence is -

- The ability to recognise, understand and manage our own emotions, and

- The ability to recognise, understand and influence the emotions of others

What does this mean to you personally ?

What does this mean with your relationships with others

We have looked at understanding your own personality type, which is the first step in building your emotional intelligence. The next steps are about putting that knowledge and awareness into practice. In order to have a wider idea of self awareness you need to know things like what motivates you, what triggers you, or working out as we discussed in book 1 , what your values are.

Take your time and fill out the following -

What is your understanding of self awareness?

Are you aware of your goals? - immediate and long term, what are they ?

What are your values, those things that you hold dear to you?

What are your drivers (motivators)?

Emotional Triggers - what does this mean to you? - Do you have
any examples?

Once you have an idea of your own self awareness the next step is to have an idea of how you manage yourself. For example, if you have a boundary or value that someone disrespects, how do you react?. As survivors we sometimes have issues respecting our own boundaries - how do you react when you feel you have let yourself down?. Do you retreat into yourself and say nothing so as to not upset anyone or do you fly into a blind rage. If you have a goal that you are aiming for but not achieving, what do you do? Give up? Or re-evaluate the time you've given yourself to achieve it ? If someone is upsetting you, how do you manage your reaction?

What is your understanding of Self Management

What are situations that could cause an emotional reaction ?

When we are looking at developing our self management, one of the things that we need to be aware of is our reaction time. This is the time it takes for something to happen and how long it takes us to respond. Quite often, especially for toxic relationships, hurtful things can be said like being told that you 'should be over it by now ' or someone telling you that they don't believe you.

This kind of response and behaviour can be very emotive for us and can result in us reacting very quickly and often in the wrong way. For some of us - we rage. We scream and shout at the indignity of not being believed. For others we shrink and become small and allow the other person to believe that they are right. Neither of these reactions are correct and do not actually serve us in the long term. What we need to learn is an appropriate reaction time and response when we can calmly and unemotionally state the facts of what happened.

What would you need to consider and do to be effective at self management?

Write down your definition of 'Self Motivation'

What do you have to do to motivate yourself? How do you convince yourself to do something?

How do you stay motivated or stay on track when become emotionally withdrawn from something

Do you stick at everything ? What is the emotional result if you don't ?

What is the emotional result if you do ?

What Self Talk could you benefit from starting?

A lot of people, myself included, struggle to answer questions about how we manage ourselves. In truth, we tend to not think about it or even be consciously aware of such a concept. This isn't just survivors - it's every one. Self management should be called self motivation in a lot of ways. It is about having an understanding that if we are aware of and control our emotional state, we are more likely to get an outcome that rewards us. Everyone is motivated by reward. The problem is that sometimes that reward is not always obvious or it can seem far away. For example, in book 1 I talked about how to do affirmations. I talked about how to choose the right affirmations for you, How to feel when you say them and even how to word them. The motivation for doing them is that in time you will change your own self beliefs and increase your self esteem, but because that reward of a better mindset is not instant, it becomes easier to give up. It becomes a problem of what you want most - to overcome what the trauma has done or to change your habits and keep at something. For some it is about rewarding themselves to keep them self motivated. In this example it may be that for every week they fully complete their affirmations, they treat themselves to a luxury hot chocolate or whatever takes fancy. Our ultimate motivation should be to either change the negative emotions and mindset that have been ingrained by abuse or to stop other people making us feel that way. Either by getting them to understand and stop what they and respect our boundaries, or to remove them from our life.

Step three of building your emotional intelligence is the awareness of others.We have already touched on this by getting you to look at the colour personality type of other people in your life. In order to build the meaningful connections in our lives - which is something we all yearn, we need to be aware others

What is your understanding of 'others awareness'? How quickly do you judge or assume about others ?

What could you do/ have you done to show that you are aware of other people in your life

How could an emotionally intelligent warrior use awareness of others?

How can you demonstrate 'Active Listening?'

How would you describe the above words?

Apathy -

Empathy -

Sympathy

How can you demonstrate Empathy? What would you physically/
verbally do for each -

Listen Actively

Body Language

Tone of Voice

Eye Contact

Choice of words

Line of questioning

Give Them Time

Being present in a conversation

How do all these change if you are going through a bad day or
feeling that inner child ?

How can using the previous personality colors help you be 'others aware'

Now that we have looked at Self Awareness, Self Management and Awareness of other people, it's time to look at our relationships and how we interact with others and how we can influence both relationships and conversations when we put this awareness in practice.

What is your understanding of Relationships

One of the final pieces of the puzzle increasing our emotional intelligence is the state that each party is in when it comes to having a conversation. There are three states that we can be in. PARENT, ADULT and CHILD. This is true of every single person on the planet and depending on what state each person is in at the time, will dictate how a conversation goes or if it is going to be beneficial. It does not matter if you are dealing with a toxic person or you are trying to build a friendship or even a romantic interest . Ideally to get the best out of a relationship or conversation you want to be in an adult state of mind and you want the other person to be in an adult state of mind as well. This is where people have an exchange and a mutual understanding. Even if that understanding is agreeing to disagree. Adult to adult conversations have mutual trust and respect. What tends to happen, more so with toxic relationships is that one person normally assumes the parent role which instantly makes the other person assume the role of the child. That person is going to be us- the one who was abused. Assuming the child role is not to be confused with the inner child or doing inner child work. This is not about getting in touch with emotions. This is about identifying how we react to people and how we can get people to react to us. For many of us it is very easy to want respect, to be believed and to feel validated by another person. Let's say for example (because it's a real example for many) that a parent doesn't believe that their child was abused. The person who was abused and is a grown adult will get annoyed with their parents. They for validation, for belief, for comfort, but because we enter that conversation already on the back foot of being in child state - the other person will do one of two things. They either enter the child state as well and meet you on that level or, what more commonly happens, the other person slips into the parent state. The problem is that the parent that did believe you when you first told them, will still give you the same response now as they both assume roles of parent and child. In either case the conversation becomes emotive, draining and a waste of time. It doesn't help heal us and if anything just reinforces our lack of self worth. If the same person went into that conversation and assumed an ADULT state and had the conversation adult to adult. It would be very different. It would not become about needing validation or being believed. It would not be about needing anything from the other person at all. It becomes about stating facts and requests for change. The tricky part is keeping the other person in the adult state - and what is even trickier is not slipping or allowing ourselves to be dragged into the opposing state. This comes back to self awareness and noticing that if the other person is slipping into child state and you feel yourself slipping into parent state (because it can happen that way round as well) then stop the conversation and take a breather. Exactly the same if they slip onto their parent state and you slip into child state. If you are not sure if someone is slipping into a non adult state have a look at the negative traits of their personality colour. Also listen to how they are making you feel. If it is not on even ground, then they are changing the playing field.

So how can you help influence the way in which someone will react? Well aside from that emotional state of remaining in adult mode, you state things as fact in an unemotional way.

' I was abused' when stated calmly is less likely to invoke a reaction from someone than

'I WAS abused' or 'I was ABUSED'.

Even though they are the same words, stating as fact will invoke an adult to adult conversation. Putting emphasis on words is demanding belief and will instantly put you in child state whilst putting the other person in adult state.

Words that you use can also dictate the direction of state a person can be in. For example the word 'Blame' can put someone in a child state. However using words such as ' I hold you responsible' or ' I hold you accountable' puts a much different spin on it and will hold a person in adult mode for longer.

Think about a toxic person in your life. Write down the things you want to them. Is this coming from a child state? How could you reword it so that it comes from an adult state?

How can you influence your relationships with -
Your family -

Your Friends

Your therapist

Your Spouse

Now that you have completed those exercises (I did warn you there were a lot), you should have a greater understanding of your self awareness, but more importantly you should also have an understanding of other people and what makes them tick and how they operate. This knowledge , when used properly , will give you an advantage to navigate and influence conversations. If you have to have a difficult conversation for example, like telling your partner about being abused as a child. That can be one of the hardest conversations in the world to have. But it can be made easier by preempting how the other person will react. If you other half is a green personality type then they will want to hug and cuddle you and offer reassurance. If they are red, they may fly into an instant rage. If they are a blue personality type, they may want to ask lots of details and have questions and if they are yellow they may portray signs of extreme disbelief and shock. By knowing yourself and the other person, you have the advantage of knowing what your needs are and also be able to prepare for their reaction, ie-if your spouse is a very blue personality and wants details, then be prepared to share as many details as you have to hand. It is also important to remember that most people do not actually do this sort of work on themselves. They generally have no idea of their own level of emotional intelligence (or lack of) or self awareness, so whilst you can take the driving seat and explain things to them on their level, you need to remember that they may not be able to do the same in return. But when and if you get to being able to disclose your abuse, you also need to remember that although this is a very old and deep scar for you, for them it may be very new. This is especially important to remember if a conversation gets too much and you need it to stop. It can be easy to get pulled into the conversation deeper and deeper, when you actually - you need it to stop or calm down. At times, as survivors we all need to remember that we need to have that element of self care and compassion and ask for a conversation to stop , or some time to think or breath. It comes back to that 'reaction time' piece.

Other ways in which emotional intelligence is useful is with toxic people in our lives. Many survivors have at least one toxic person in their life. For me it was my Mum. When I initially told her I was abused as a kid I was thirty seven years old. I had had a difficult and estranged relationship with her for many years. Before the day I had told her I had not seen her in well over fifteen years. She has never even met her youngest grandson. I tracked her down to tell her that I was abused as a kid and to tell her what happened to me. When I first did this, I was not in control of my emotions or had any sense of self awareness. My mother's reaction when I told her about the abuse was to rage. She blamed my dad - because I was in his care at the time. She blamed my siblings for not looking out for me, my nan and even me for not speaking up. I told her that it didn't just happen in my dad's care. It also happened whenI was in her care and that I was raped at fourteen by one of her co-workers on the farm she worked on. That was also my fault for not staying away from him. My mother's personality type is very yellow. If you look at the previous table with the personality traits , you will see that a ' Yellow ' will attack under pressure. My mother was attacking everyone and everything at that point and because i was not emotionally in control or even aware at that point, I was shrinking- to the point where I was slowly sliding under the table I was sitting at. For weeks after I told her I started getting random phone calls from her at work. She had found my workplace number and would call every other week. She would tell me how she couldn't believe how one of her children had been abused, whilst still maintaining that if everyone else had looked after me properly it wouldn't have happened. One of the reasons that I initially went to tell my mum was to not only tell her of the abuse but to also tell her that I hold her accountable for it. Or at least large parts of it. She may not have been directly responsible for the sexual abuse, but she was emotionally and physically absent, and it was a lot of her actions and decisions in life that led to me being sexually abused.

The second time I visited her (it was about nine months later) I was much more emotionally aware of myself. She asked how I was and how the court case was going. By that point I had looked for my cousin on facebook. I had had that wanting and needing to know what his life was like. I hadn't seen him since I was sixteen. I found his profile and saw that we had one mutual friend. But as I scrolled his newsfeed, I saw that he had a lot of contact with our mutual friend's son. He was eight. I went to the police station to safeguard the boy but I couldn't tell them my suspicions without telling them why I thought he was in danger. So after I gave my statement, the officer i was talking to asked me one simple question ' Do I want to press charges?'; and a quiet little voice in me said 'yes'. Since I had given my statement the police had interviewed allsorts of people. Disclosure witnesses such as my wife and friends and people who were in my life at the time such as parents. My mum had already been interviewed when I knocked on her door. Something I was not aware of having happened yet. But she asked how the court case was going and then informed me that the police had visited her and took a statement and that she had told them that she couldn't tell them anything because she didn't know anything. She looked at me and said the words ' Well I wasn't in your life when you were nine, so it's your dad's fault'. Those words hit me hard. And deep. Thankfully, by that time I was more emotionally aware because she said those words and even before I could say what I wanted to say I could feel myself shrinking. I looked her square in the eye and asked her ' Do you think that if you bothered to stick around it might not have happened?'. I knew that the only way I was going to get through this conversation was to be direct with her. Otherwise she would have overpowered me and just blamed everyone and everything else. Don't get me wrong, it was not easy and if you ever have one of these conversations - it will not be easy.

My heart was pounding and having this conversation felt as hard if not harder than giving my statement to the police. She stopped and looked at me and I calmly and directly told her all the things I wanted to tell her the first time I visited. I told her how it was her that moved her boyfriend in the house when I was five that used to be physically aggressive to us both. It was her sleeping around that split our family up. It was her that moved me around the country and ostracized me from every family member except her for years - to the point I couldn't remember them. It was her that kept me isolated. It was her that gave me up at court. She objected to that one. She had always insisted that she lost the custody case for me against my dad. However, my dad had kept all the court records for the custody case. I had never read them before I gave my statement to the police. I didn't even know they existed. But in order to give some clarification on dates my dad gave them to me. My mother stood there and told me that she lost custody and that is why I went to live with my dad. That's what I had believed since I was nine. The court documents however told me exactly that she gave up on the case and then how she relocated 100 miles away. I told her how it was exactly her actions that led her youngest child in a vulnerable position and open to being abused. I told her that I hold her accountable and that I did not want her in my life and that she is not to contact me.

If it had not been for doing the self work on my emotional intelligence,I would not have had that conversation. At least not in the calm and 'matter of fact' way that I did and not in the direct manner that she needed to hear it; and certainly not in an adult to adult manner

If you need to have a conversation with someone toxic in your life and you are not sure how to handle it, then I work out what colour personality type that person is. As mentioned, most people do not work on their emotional intelligence, and so it is best trying to have a difficult conversation on their level. If you are a blue person who is very into logic and facts and you are trying to tell a person who is very yellow exuberant , the yellow person will instantly dismiss what you are saying. If you are a very green personality type and need comfort and calm, then taking that approach with a red personality type who is very direct and blunt will not work. If you don't take the time to adapt a little to the other person, the message will be lost in translation and you will never get through to the other person. Just remember that you need to remain in that adult state and can stop the conversation whenever you like.

As survivors of childhood trauma, learning to identify and connect with our emotions is one of the hardest parts of healing. We have to learn to parent and regulate ourselves in this area as we learn to navigate our way through our healing journeys. The reward of going through the pain of connecting with the inner child and allowing your emotions to be felt and and honoured, and to grow in this area is one of the biggest steps you can take on the path to healing.

Boundaries

Now that you have begun to work on your emotional intelligence and self awareness, setting boundaries with people should be a lot easier

All survivors of childhood abuse have issues setting healthy boundaries. Because we grew up and learned that we can only be validated by pleasing other people, we carry that belief into adulthood. And so, that's what we continue to do. Even when we do not want to do something. Even when it makes us unhappy. Sometimes even when we know it is wrong or illegal. We develop very blurry boundaries and allow people (and sometimes ourselves) to trample all over them in order to make other either people happy or to avoid the anxiety and pain of being scolded and being made to feel less than. Having little or no boundaries can manifest itself in many ways. For me it manifested in the hatred of the idea of letting other people down. I used to go along with others' plans and ideas because I did not want to upset them. Which would consequently mean that I would miss out on things that I wanted to do. I would have such a fear of being rejected or abandoned if I didn't go along with other people's plans that it would almost cripple me. I was a victim and prisoner of my own insecurities. But that is not the only way that a lack of boundaries can manifest.

It may be that you are continuously going from bad relationship to bad relationship, it may be that you are really bad at making a decision and settling for others making them for you. (This is how a lot of trauma victims end up inviting a consistent stream of controlling narcissists into their lives) It may be that you are constantly annoyed with yourself and tired for no apparent reason.

It may be that because you have no boundaries you overshare private and personal information without thought about who you are sharing it with. Or it may be that you are constantly the victim - and if the words ' 'Why is it always me?' have ever left your lips then you definitely do not set good boundaries

Having a lack of boundaries can manifest itself in many ways.

But you are a survivor. A warrior. And you are going to learn and grow.

We have done a big chunk of the work by identifying your self awareness. This, combined with learning about your values in book 1 will give you all the tools you need to set your boundaries with people.

So how do you actually set a boundary? Well firstly you need to set your limits. You need to decide what you are going to physically ,mentally, emotionally and spiritually allow in your life. If you are not sure then give it some thought and write a list. If you are not sure where you stand on a subject or activity, then tune into your feelings. If someone is asking you to do something or putting you in a position where you are either feeling discomfort or resentment then it is not for you.

Secondly - and this is an important factor. Give yourself permission to draw up a boundary. Give yourself permission to say 'NO!'. Give yourself permission to be direct and tell the other person that you do not want to or that they are crossing the line. Then go ahead and do it. Just remember that you need to be self aware when doing it and you need to state your boundary from that adult state of being.

It doesn't matter if it's a friend asking you to participate in something you don't want to do, or if it is a toxic person that you need to set up boundaries with, even if that boundary is cutting them from your life. The rules are the same. Give yourself permission to have the boundary in place and from an adult state of mind be assertive and direct and tell them where your line is. Tell them what it is that you do not want or will not accept.

And that's it.

If the other person respects you, they will respect what you are asking and comply. If they do not respect you are saying then you need to decide if that is a person you want in your life.

But only you can decide that.

Only you can choose your boundaries and only you can enforce them.

But by doing the work it does get better

And you will be a stronger warrior.

Note about the Author

Mike Bowles is a survivor of childhood abuse. He endured most of his childhood living with emotional, physical and sexual, something that will be with him forever. Like most survivors of abuse he had suppressed the memories of his abuse for many years. It was only as he approached the age of thirty-seven that he began to recall the details of his childhood in the form of flashbacks. He quickly developed severe anxiety and depression and post traumatic stress disorder. After being signposted eleven times by various sexual abuse charities and therapists(each claiming that because he was 'not a woman or lived as a woman', they could not help him) he decided to go onto a path of self healing whilst he endured an eighteen month waiting list for a therapist. In that time he began to study the psychology of what happens to abused and traumatised children in order to understand what was happening to him. He then moved onto trialling every method of healing that he could find from a variety of fields including psychology, holistic therapies and even life coaching models.

Today he heads world wide trauma groups online, helping thousands of childhood abuse victims heal from their trauma with the methods that he has learned and put into practice in his own healing journey to move from victim to survivor to warrior.

Leave A Review

If you have purchased this book from Amazon, and you have found the exercises in it useful, then please leave a review. This will help other survivor's also find the book and maybe get some help that they may be struggling to find elsewhere.

Keep an eye out for Book 2 - The Inner Child, Emotional Intelligence and Boundaries